The Ancient Jewish

CROSS

Al Garza PhD, Th.D

Table of Content

Introduction

𝓗ow many times have you looked around the stores,

television or even at your friends and noticed them and the people

wearing a cross around there neck? Yet they have no clue what it is

that they are wearing. Most of the time they have no religious belief

or faith that they confess yet they wear the cross as a mere fashion

statement. Celebrities and music people on television wear crosses

around there neck as if they understand the meaning behind it. When

asked about the cross they wear, they simply reply that it looks good

with what they wear and like how it looks. Most people today have

lost the true understanding and meaning behind the cross. They don't

know that it has its roots in ancient Judaism before Yeshua (Jesus).

That the ancient cross is before the Persians who killed and crucified

people on wooden crosses.

The ancient Hebrews used the image of the cross as part of

their alphabet before the Hebrew alphabet was changed to the

classical Hebrew script after the Babylonian captivity which remains

unchanged today. The ancient Jews understood the image of the

cross as part of their alphabet. The cross was the image, letter and symbol called the "Taw" or the "Tav", in Modern Hebrew, and it was the pictograph used before the Babylonian captivity. The ancient cross, the Taw, was used to mean "mark", "sign", "covenant" and "seal". Today Jewish Rabbi's have stopped using this ancient symbol because of the use of it in Christianity. They want to have nothing in common with Christianity and Yeshua (Jesus) even though the cross, the Taw, is part of their ancient pictograph script. We as followers of Yeshua (Jesus) have to come back to the true meaning of the cross and its place in ancient Judaism. We must never forget why Yeshua (Jesus), the Jewish Messiah, had to die on a cross and what it meant to all mankind. The true meaning of the cross and its Jewish roots in the Hebrew alphabet has to be understood if we are to take up the cross and follow Yeshua (Jesus). The cross you wear around your neck is a Jewish symbol and image which means "sign, covenant, and seal of YHWH God". It represents our Jewish roots and faith in the Messiah Yeshua (Jesus) who was crucified on the cross and sealed and finalized the covenant on it by his blood. The cross is our sign and mark that shows we follow the resurrected Yeshua (Jesus).

*"And he who does not take his **cross** and follow after Me is not worthy of Me."* **Yeshua, Matthew 10:38**

In this book you will discover the true meaning behind the ancient letter and symbol of the cross. The final covenant and promise made to the Jewish people which was completed by the shedding of the Messiah's blood on the cross and gave man the opportunity to put their faith in Yeshua (Jesus) for the forgiveness of their sins. Both Jew and Gentile become one man through the Messiah Yeshua (Jesus) and by the message of the cross which is the power God. We bare the mark and sign of God which is the Taw cross that all believers receive when they believe.

Chapter 1

Understanding Ancient Hebrew

Word Pictures

When ancient Hebrew was first written, each letter

represented both a sound and a picture. In Chinese and in ancient

Egyptian every word is formed by adding pictures together to draw

out the meaning of the word. This was also done in the ancient

Hebrew; a word picture is a word that is described by pictures. Let

us look at the entire Hebrew alphabet in the form of the pictograph

script:

The entire Hebrew alphabet was written in picture form, from Alef

to Tav. The last letter and picture being the Tav is the picture of the

cross. So if the Hebrews wanted to write a word using the pictures they would place them together and use the meaning of both pictures to communicate. For example, if they wanted to say "father" in Hebrew they would say "Ab". Now using the pictures they would put "Alef" and "Bet" together to say "Ab" or "father". Now let's look deeper into the meaning of the word "father" in Hebrew. View chart below.

Name	Pictograph	Meaning	Name	Pictograph	Meaning
Aleph		Ox / strength / leader	Lamed		Staff / goad / control / "toward"
Bet		House / "In"	Mem		Water / chaos
Gimmel		Foot / camel / pride	Nun		Seed / fish / activity / life
Dalet		Tent door / pathway	Samekh		Hand on staff / support / prop
Hey		Lo! Behold! "The"	Ayin		Eye / to see / experience
Vav		Nail / peg / add / "And"	Pey		Mouth / word / speak
Zayin		Plow / weapon / cut off	Tsade		Man on side / desire / need
Chet		Tent wall / fence / separation	Qof		Sun on horizon / behind
Tet		Basket / snake / surround	Resh		Head / person / first
Yod		Arm and hand / work / deed	Shin		Eat / consume / destroy
Kaf		Palm of hand / to open	Tav		Mark / sign / covenant

In the chart above you can see that the "Alef" is the picture of an ox or bull and the "Bet" is a picture of a house. The ox represents strength and leader while "Bet" represents a picture of a house.

So together the word "Ab" means "father, leader of the house.", that is exactly what the scriptures teach about the father being the head of the house and the leader. Below you will see the chart for the word picture for both "father" and "God" and in Classical Hebrew.

"Word Picture"		Classical Hebrew	
Pictograph	Meaning	Hebrew	Meaning
ᴜ ᑲ	Strong Leader	אֵל	Name for God; "Strength." Used 250 times in the *Tanakh*.
ᒪ ᑲ	Strength (of the) house	אָב	Father

The name for "God" in Hebrew is "El" and as you can see above the word picture means "God, the strong leader". This is how the ancient Hebrews wrote and communicated using word pictures. Now let us look at how the Hebrew language has evolved in Modern Hebrew.

Hebrew *(Ivrit:* עברית*)* is the name given to one of the world's oldest languages. The name derives from Eber *('ever)* (עבר), the son of Shem; *'ever* means "region across or beyond" and derives from a root that means to pass over. Shem is called אבי כל־בני־עבר, "the father of all of the sons of Eber" (Gen 10:21); and therefore Hebrew descendants are called Semites. In the Scriptures, Hebrew is used as an adjective (עברי) to describe Jews who are "from the other side" (i.e., of the Euphrates River). Modern Hebrew is called *Ivrit.*

In Genesis 31:47, Laban and Jacob refer to a heap of stones in their native speech. Laban uses the phrase "Yegar Sahaduta" which is Aramaic, but Jacob uses (גלעד) "Gal-Ed" which is Hebrew. The Garden of Eden, or *gan eden* (גן־עדן) is known as the first paradise, the location for the origin of man made *b'tzelem elohim,* in the image of God. This image included the ability to use a God-given language (a theory that an original source language was given in Eden is called "Edenics"). Man was exiled from Eden, however, and began to be dispersed upon the face of the earth. The Great Flood, or *mabul* (מבול) effected judgment upon the antediluvian clans for their constant wickedness before YHWH, the only survivors were the direct descendants of the clan of Noach. The Toldot b'nei Noach (the generations of Noah, or Table of 70 Nations as listed in Genesis 10) indicates some of the earliest migration of clans. Noah's son Shem is also called אבי כל־בני־עבר, "the father of all of the sons of Eber" (Gen 10:21); his toldot is given in Genesis 11:10. The Tower of Babel, or *migdal bavel* (מגרל בבל) located in the "plains of Shinar" of ancient Mesopotamia (Gen 11:1-9) is historically identified as the original site of ancient Babylon. Perhaps the tower was a form of idolatrous ziggurat meant to unify the ancients.

Abraham, a descendant of the clan of Eber, was called by God from Ur of the Chaldees (i.e., *kasdim)* in 1800 BCE to the land of Canaan. The language in Canaan at that time has been called "proto-Canaanite," the parent language of the dialects of Hittites, Amorites, Hivites, Jebusites, Perizites. In relation to the Hebrews, proto-Canaanite script may be called *ketav Ivri.*

During the 400 years that Abraham's clan was in Egypt (Genesis 15:13), the Hebrews still spoke a Canaanite variant (e.g. Yoseph's brothers in Egypt: see Genesis 42:23). An article of orthodox Jewish faith is that God originally revealed the Torah to Mosheh using *Ketav Ashurit* (from *ashrei)*, not *ketav Ivri,* since the earlier script was considered profane and riddled with paganism. After Mosheh broke the first set of tablets, however, God wrote the second set using the profane script. After the Babylonian captivity, ketav Ashurit was fully restored to the Jewish people by Ezra the Scribe and came to be called *Lashon HaKodesh* (the holy language). This same script has been used until this day for the writing of Torah scrolls. Modern soferut (scribal arts) include the Bet Yosef, Bet Ari, and Sephard styles of ketav Ashurit for Sifrei Torah (torah scrolls).

A Midrash on the *Migdal Bavel* (Tower of Babel) teaches that at the end of time all people will once again speak one language and that will be a purified form of the Hebrew tongue. There is also d'rash on the verse: "For then I will make the peoples pure of speech, so that they all invoke YHWH by name and serve Him with one accord" (Zeph 3:9) that indicates the same.

Now let us look at the charts below and at how the Hebrew alphabet changed throughout the centuries.

kaf	yod	tet	chet	zayin	vav	hey	dalet	gimmel	bet	'alef

tav	shin	resh	qof	tsade	pey	'ayin	samech	nun	mem	lamed

Proto-Canaanite Pictographs

ḥēt	zayin	wāw	hē	dālet	gīmel	bēt	'ālef
ḥ	z	w	h	d	g	b	'

sāmek	nun	mēm	lāmed	kaf	yōd	ṭēt
s	n	m	l	k	y	ṭ

tāw	śin/šin	rēš	qōf	ṣādē	pē	'ayin
t	š	r	q	ṣ	p	'

The Phoenician Script

Proto Hebrew Script

kaf	yod	tet	chet	zayin	vav	he	dalet	gimel	bet	alef
k	y	t	h	z	w	h	d	g	b	'

tav	shin	resh	kof	tzadi	pe	ayin	samech	nun	mem	lamed
t	sh	r	k	tz	p	'	s	n	m	l

The Samaritan Script

kaf	yod	tet	chet	zayin	vav	hey	dalet	gimmel	bet	'alef

tav	shin	resh	qof	tsade	pey	'ayin	samech	nun	mem	lamed

Classical Hebrew Script

kaf	yod	tet	chet	zayin	vav	he	dalet	gimel	bet	alef
tav	shin/sin	resh	kof	tzadi(k)	pe	ayin	samech	nun	mem	lamed

Modern Hebrew Cursive

kaf	yod	tet	chet	zayin	vav	he	dalet	gimel	bet	alef
tav	shin/sin	resh	kof	tzadi(k)	pe	ayin	samech	nun	mem	lamed

Rashi-Style Hebrew

The Rashi style is used mainly to write commentaries on texts. It is named in honor of Rabbi Shlomo Yitzchaki (1040-1105 AD) a.k.a. Rashi, one of the greatest medieval Jewish scholars and bible commentators.

There are some scholars who divide the Hebrew language into four basic periods.

1. **Biblical Hebrew** – aka Classical Hebrew; by the time of Jesus, Aramaic was the common language, but Hebrew was

used in synagogues and in Temple worship. Jesus knew and spoke Biblical Hebrew.

2. **Mishnaic Hebrew** – aka Rabbinic Hebrew; Talmud and Midrash; 2nd century AD. Note that the grammar and vocabulary of this Hebrew is very different than Biblical Hebrew.

3. **Medieval Hebrew** – Used to translate Arabic works into Hebrew, e.g., Maimonides and other medievalists.

4. **Modern Hebrew** – 19th century to present. Eliezar Ben Yehuda (1858-1922) led the rebirth of Hebrew as a spoken language. After immigrating to Israel in 1881, he began promoting the use of Hebrew at home and in the schools.

In Ben Yahuda's pocket dictionary we see the ancient cross that was identified with the Hebrew letter Taw.

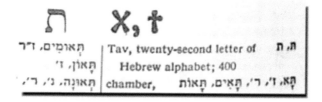

תָּאוּמִים, ז"ר	Tav, twenty-second letter of	ת ,תּ
תָּאוֹן, ז'	Hebrew alphabet; 400	
תָּאוּנָה, נ' ,ר'.	chamber, תָּאוֹת ,תָּאִים ,ר' ,ז"ת,	

As you can see from the scripts above, every Taw is the cross from the Proto-Canaanite script to the Samaritan script. The history of the ancient Hebrew letter Taw being the image or picture of the cross is solid. Every Hebrew scholar knows this. The Jewish and Gentile Christians did not adapt a pagan symbol to show for their faith. They chose the ancient Jewish picture of the Taw known as the cross as their symbol for the covenant and seal of God on them.

Scholars are uncertain how far back ketav Ivri goes in Jewish history, though it appears to date to at least the 10th century BC. The work of some paleolinguists suggests that an even earlier form of Canaanite cuneiform is actually the basis of ketav Ivri. These Hebrew Word Pictures are regarded as the most ancient form of Hebrew known. Here is a simplified illustration of the progression of the script forms (left-to-right, oldest to newest):

Canaanite	Ketav Ivri	Ketav Ashurit	Modern

Chapter 2

The Hebrew Sign

Of God

When I first understood the true meaning of the cross from

the ancient Hebrew alphabet I began to remember so many versus

from both the Tanakh and from the New Covenant scriptures about

the cross and the use of the Taw. Starting from the Tanakh (Old

Testament) I remember the words of Iyob (Job), the oldest book in

the Tanakh, "Oh that I had one to hear me! See, my **mark!** Let the

Almighty answer me, and let my Accuser write an indictment." Iyob

31:35. The Hebrew word for "mark" is "Taw", the very word that is

represented by the image or symbol of the cross. Iyob literally says,

"See, my Taw†ʺ, the very image of the cross. Iyob invokes the very

mark that represents his faith in the Almighty and proclaims that the

Almighty answer him because of the "mark" which is literally the

cross. We must also remember that this "mark" was not a literal

"mark" but a spiritual one that reflects back to Yehezqel 9. (Ezekiel)

In Yehezqel (Ezekiel) we read the following:

"Walk through the city of Jerusalem and **mark** *the forehead of anyone who is truly upset and sad about the disgusting things that are being done here. He turned to the other six men and said,*

"Follow him and put to death everyone who doesn't have a **mark** *on their forehead. Show no mercy or pity! Kill men and women, parents and children. Begin here at my temple and be sure not to harm those who are* **marked**. *The men immediately killed the leaders who were standing there."*

YHWH God commanded the man in linen with a writers ink horn to put a "mark" or more literally in the Hebrew, the Taw ✝, the very image of the cross on their foreheads. We know from history that it was the Babylonians who, during Yehezqel's time, were the ones who conquered Israel and destroyed the Temple with fire. Yehezqel was describing the spiritual judgment that fell on Israel because of their apostasy. The very "mark" was a cross that would separate the true Jewish believers in the God of Israel from the unbelievers who had turned their back on Him. These were the leaders of Israel who worshiped the Sun and desecrated the temple of God. This practice of putting a "mark" or the "cross" on the forehead is still practiced today in the Catholic Church. It is called Ash Wednesday and many Catholic believers place a cross image on their foreheads made from ash right before the celebration of the day of the resurrection, better know as Easter. This has been a tradition of the Catholic Church since the 11th century where women were the first to put a cross made of ashes on their foreheads. The men later adopted this practice. The understanding of this practice has its place in the Tanakh and in the prophet Yehezqel (Ezekiel) who saw the man in linen "mark" out on their foreheads the image of the cross to those who did not turn their back on YHWH. YHWH God commanded that they should not be harmed and that they should not face His judgment which was to come upon the people of Israel through the Babylonian captivity. Many Jews were killed during that time but the ones who were faithful to the God of Israel and who were "marked" out by God with the Taw cross were spared.

*"Follow him and put to death everyone who doesn't have a **mark** on their **forehead**. Show no mercy or pity! Kill men and women, parents and children. Begin here at my temple and be sure **not to harm those who are marked.**"* Yehezqel 9:6

We must not forget that YHWH God shows mercy to those

who remain faithful to Him and who do not turn their back on Him in unbelief. The ancient Jewish scholars understood this, who in the Jewish Talmud said that the mark put on the foreheads in Yehezqel 9 was the ancient Hebrew letter Taw, the last letter of the Hebrew alphabet. This was recorded in Shabbat 55a of the Jewish Talmud. This mark would have been understood to be the image of the cross, see pictures below.

The image on the Jewish coin in the 2nd century A.D. shows the Hebrew letter Taw in the shape of the cross. This was the clear understanding of the ancient Hebrew letter.

One of the most noteworthy uses of the Taw cross is found in the columns of the Great Isaiah Scroll. Eleven ancient Taw crosses were written in the margins to point out Messianic portions of the scroll. They were looked at as slanting crosses. Scholars teach that these marks could be read as a Greek X chi, this refers to the Greek word Christos or Christ, the Greek word for the Hebrew Messiah.

To read more on this go to The Archaeology of the New Testament pages 346-348.

Some of the passages that contain the slanted cross in the margins are found in Yeshayahu (Isaiah) 2:19, 32:1, 42:1-5, 42:19, 44:26, 55:3-4, 56:13, and 66:5. There are others, each one referred to as Messianic passages. In the margins of each of the passages you can see the slanted cross that represents Messianic texts.

Ancient Hebrew Taw / Tav / Tof

The Jewish believers continued the teaching of the Jewish leaders and accepted the Jewish symbols of the Chi X and the Taw cross as their own.

The Essene Community at Qumran was famous for the Dead Sea Scroll. Much has be learned about them over the last number of decades. The letter Taw played a significant role in their understanding of what it meant to be marked as one of God's people and as a symbol for the coming Messiah. When the Essenes baptized their own converts they were marked on the foreheads with a Taw cross. The convert was considered a part of the faithful remnant that would be spared in the coming day of God's wrath. The Jewish Community stopped using the ancient letter Taw to anoint with oil and as a symbol of their identity soon after the Messianic Jews and early Christians took it up as part of their faith in Yeshua (Jesus). The Jewish Encyclopedia states:

It is not unlikely that, owing to their opposition to the Christian cross, the Jewish interpreters adopted the kaph form instead of the X, the original Taw of Ezek. 9:4

The cross and the Chi were originally Jewish symbols until the Church began to use them. Jewish rituals were changed because the followers of Yeshua (Jesus) applied the Taw cross to the cross that Yeshua (Jesus) died on. They failed to realize that the cross that Yeshua died on was the covenant Taw cross that would be used to represent the new mark and sign for the believer. We read in Hazon (Revelation) 7:2-8 that the 144,000 Jewish servants of God are sealed with the "seal of the Living God" on their foreheads and are protected from the Judgment of God once more. This is a reference to Yehezqel (Ezekiel) 9 that Yohanan (John) makes. The fact remains that the Taw cross was and still is very Jewish. The ancient Taw cross remains marked in Jewish history.

Chapter 3

Yeshua (Jesus) And The

Taw

*W*hat we have learned so far is that the ancient Hebrew

alphabet is not the same as the Modern Hebrew alphabet. The

original Hebrew letters were all pictures used to form words. The

question now is what role did the Hebrew letter pictures play in

regards to Yeshua (Jesus)? We must first understand that just like the

prophecies concerning the Messiah in the Tanakh (Old Testament)

did not literally say this was about Yeshua (Jesus), the Hebrew

picture letters do not literally say that this is about Yeshua (Jesus)

either. What they do reveal, just like the Tanakh prophecies of the

Messiah, is a clearer understanding of the sacrifice and redemptive

plan of Yeshua (Jesus) after the fact. When the ancient Taw cross is

combined with other picture letters in the ancient Hebrew alphabet

something revealing is discovered. The veil is moved to see and

understand that YHWH God had put his redemptive plan in the

very language he created for his Jewish people. YHWH has preserved his language and in it He has preserved the testimony of the work of Yeshua the Jewish Messiah and his role from the foundation of the world. When Yeshua (Jesus) died on the cross, he died on the ancient Hebrew symbol for covenant. The combining form of the Hebrew picture letters with the Taw cross is just the beginning.

There are times when the letter or word has a clear message for us. This is the case with the last letter of the Hebrew alphabet. Taw which literally means the sign of the covenant or mark of the covenant is spelled in Modern Hebrew תו. The first letter that is used to spell out Taw in Hebrew is the picture of the cross while the second letter in the word, waw or vav in Modern Hebrew, is the picture of a nail, see chart in chapter 1. When we look at the fact that the very word for sign, covenant and mark in Hebrew is a picture of a cross and a nail, this carries a powerful prophetic significance. We can now better understand the Apostle Sha'ul (Paul) in his letter to the Qolasim (Colossians) when he says, *"having blotted out the handwriting of ordinances that was against us, which was contrary to us, and He has taken it out of the way, **nailing** it to **the cross.**"*

This is a clear reference to the very word of the Taw which is spelled out in ancient Hebrew with the picture of a cross and a nail. Shall we believe that this is all a coincidence or that the God of Israel preserved, within the ancient Hebrew language, the true redemptive plan of salvation through the Messiah Yeshua (Jesus)?

Another word in Hebrew that has meaning in the Hebrew pictograph (word pictures) script with the Taw cross is the word "truth". The Hebrew word for "truth" is אֱמֶת (emet) and since there is 28 letters in the classical Hebrew alphabet we can see how this Hebrew word for "truth" is significant. Jesus declared, *"I am the way, **the truth**, and the life. No one comes to the Father except through Me."* The first letter in Hebrew word for "truth" is the Aleph and the second letter is the middle letter in the Hebrew alphabet Mem while the last letter of the word is the Taw. The first, middle and last letters in the Hebrew alphabet make the Hebrew word "truth" (emet) which the Jewish sages say means that the "truth" (emet) contains everything from Aleph to Taw (beginning to end). Yeshua (Jesus) is not only the way but he is the complete truth found even in the very language of the ancient Hebrew alphabet. This now brings us the Greek phrase, Alpha and Omega.

In the last letter in the New Covenant scriptures Yeshua

(Jesus) declared himself to be the Alpha and Omega, the first and the

last, the beginning and the end. See the reference in Hazon

(Revelation) 22:13. In Hebrew Yeshua would have said that he is the

Aleph and the Taw, the rishon (first) and the acharon (last), the rosh

(beginning) and the sof (end). The Aleph and the Taw have a strong

reference not only to Yeshayahu (Isaiah) 44:6 but also to Bereshith

(Genesis) 1:1. Here is how it looks in the Hebrew scripts.

Genesis 1:1

ʘ٩٦yⱷ †ʘY ᴟᴟ⅃ᴟᴟuⱷ †ʘ ᴟᴟⱷʘUⱷ ᴚʘ⅄ †⊣ᴚᴚʘᴚʘ	Canaanite
ⱳ٩ᴚ₹ Ⴟᴚᴟ ᴟᴚᴟⱳᴡ₹ Ⴟᴚ ᴟᴚ₹ᴗᴚ ᴚ٩٩ Ⴟᴚwᴚ٩٩	Ketav Ivri
ץראה תאו םימשה תא םיהלא ארב תישארב	Ketav Ashurit

First thing to understand is that the Aleph and Taw in Bereshith

(Genesis) 1:1 are the bulls head and the cross in the Canaanite script.

It literally reads, "In the beginning God created Aleph/Taw (et). The

Aleph/Taw forms a unique word that functions as a direct object

marker in both Biblical and Modern Hebrew. Yeshua (Jesus) is the direct object of the Universe and the End (sof) of all of creation. Sha'ul in Qolasim (Colossians) 1:16-17 said, *"...because by Him (Yeshua) all things were created, those in the heavens and those on earth, visible and invisible, whether thrones or dominions or rulers or authorities; all things have been created through Him and for Him. And He is before all things, and in Him all things are held together."* Yeshua (Jesus) is the Aleph/Taw, the direct object marker, and the Hebrew word pictures show him as the "Leader of the strong covenant" made by him. (Reference Dani'el 9:27)

Now let us look at the Hebrew word Torah. There is no word more Jewish than the word Torah. The word Torah means the law.

תּוֹרָה

The meaning of this word can be found in the letters that form the Hebrew word that means the law. When the Hebrew letter "Hey" is placed as the last letter of the word, it means "what is revealed from". Now look at the first three Hebrew letters and what do they tell us the law comes from? The Hebrew letter "resh" means "the man" and the next letter is "waw or vav" and it means "nail" and the last Hebrew letter is of course the "taw" or the cross. So now we can see the true meaning behind the word Torah, "What is revealed from the man nailed to the cross." This is a reminder of the prophecy from Mikah 4:2, *"For **Torah** shall go forth from Zion, and the word of YHWH from Jerusalem."* Yeshua (Jesus) himself made this statement in Mattithyahu 5:17 (Matthew), *"Think not that I came to destroy the **Torah** or the prophets: I came not to destroy, but to fulfill."* Yeshua (Jesus) was going to fulfill what the Torah and the prophets had spoken about concerning him. What was revealed from the Torah was Yeshua's (Jesus') death on the cross. The ancient Hebrew word picture for Torah reveals this. This is no coincidence that Yeshua (Jesus) died on the cross and within the ancient Hebrew language we can find such meaning concerning his death. The Torah has revealed the man nailed to the cross.

Another Hebrew word to look at is the word Sabbath or Shabat in Hebrew. The meaning of this word is of course is "rest" but the Hebrew word picture tells us something deeper. The word Sha-bat uses the Hebrew letters Shin, Bet and Taw and together they form the Hebrew Sha-bat or Sabbath. If you take away the last Hebrew letter, the Taw, you have the Hebrew word "Shoov" which means "repent and return to." But repent and return to what? The cross of course! The Taw cross at the end of the word reveals the true meaning of the word Sha-bat. It literally means, "Repent and return to the cross for rest." Looking back at Shemoth (Exodus) 20:8 in the Tanakh we can see a whole new meaning to the passage. *"Remember the **Sha-bat** day, to keep it holy..."*

Taw Bet shin

There are those who don't understand the meaning behind the word Sha-bat and have turned it into a religious ritual. In times we need to look a little deeper into a word root to get the full effect of what it means. Some words are combined word forms that have meaning when they are divided into their original form. In this case the first two letters, Shin and Bet, together mean "repent and return too" while the last letter, Taw, means "covenant" or just the cross.

In the New Covenant scriptures there are many references to the cross and its true meaning once we understand its ancient use in the Hebrew language. In other times the word simply is in reference to ones own sacrifice in order to follow Yeshua (Jesus). It is after the death, burial and resurrection of Yeshua (Jesus) that we see the impact of the word. When Yeshua (Jesus) was hanging on the cross it said *"It is finished!"* What was finished? Now that we understand that the Taw cross means covenant we can see the impact of Yeshua's words. The fulfillment of the final covenant by Yeshua's death on the Taw cross was the predetermine plan of YHWH from the beginning foretold in the ancient Hebrew letter pictures. Yeshua himself said, *"This cup which is poured out for you is the new covenant in My blood."* Luqas (Luke) 22:20. Even Sha'ul knew the importance of the Taw cross when he said, *"...and might reconcile them both in one body to God through the cross, by it having put to death the enmity."* Eph'siyim (Ephesians) 2:16. Then again he says, *"... and through Him to reconcile all things to Himself, having made peace through the blood of His cross; through Him, I say, whether things on earth or things in heaven."* Qolasim (Colossians) 1:20. The final redemptive plan of God was fulfilled on the Taw cross.

Chapter 4

The Early Church

And The Taw Cross

*T*he ancient Jewish scholars understood the meaning of the

Taw cross and used it in most common rituals. The Jewish wafers

used as meal offering in the Temple were anointed with oil in shape

of the cross. The Talmud (Mas.Menachoth 74b) tells us that "The

cakes required mingling and the wafers anointing. How were they

anointed? In the form of Chi. In the form of a cross like the Greek

letter." The Talmud also teaches that the king was anointed with a

crown of oil but that the anointing of the Priest was with a Taw cross

in the form of the Greek Chi X. What about the Church Fathers after

the 1st century? Did they continue the belief and understanding of the

Taw cross?

Septimius Tertullian lived around 160 to 240 A.D and wrote

numerous apologies, works against heretics and exhortation to other

Christians. Nearly all his works were written in Latin. He converted to Christianity when he was middle aged. Tertullian served as a

presbyter in the Church at Carthage, North Africa. He believed that

God had given Yehezqel (Ezekiel) "the very form of the cross"

which he predicted would be the sign on our foreheads in the

Jerusalem of those who follow the Messiah Yeshua (Jesus). This was

the understanding even in baptism, Tertullian *Against Marcion* 3.22.

Origen was another church father who was a pupil of

Clement of Alexandria. Origen lived around 185-255 A.D. and has

been called the "father of Christian theology". He was also the most

prolific writer of the pre-Nicene church, dictating around two

thousand works. He wrote commentaries on most of the books of the

Bible. On Yehezqel (Ezekiel) 9, Origen comments that the letter Tav

bears a resemblance "to the figure of the cross" and this prophecy is

said to regard the sign made by Christians on the forehead, Origen

Selecta in Ezechielem 13.800d.

**Hebrew letter
tav at the time
of Ezekiel**
(Paleo-Hebrew)

Another historical church figure was St. Jerome a Catholic priest and an apologist. His father was Eusebius of the city of Stridon. Jerome lived around 347 to about 420 A.D. He is known for his translation of the Bible into Latin which is the Latin Vulgate today. He is recognized by the Catholic Church as a saint and as a Doctor of the Church. The Eastern Orthodox Church also recognizes him as a saint where he is called St. Jerome of Stridonium. In Jerome's translation on Yehezqel 9:4 (Ezekiel) he correctly uses the Greek Thau in the passage in place of Taw. He clearly understood the Jewish and early Christian teaching about the sign of the cross in the passage. In his commentary on the same verse he comments on the meaning of the Thau being the shape of the cross in the original Taw form. Jerome recognized the sign as signifying the Hebrew letter Taw, from which the Greek letter Tau took its shape and name.

Centuries later in 1215 A.D. Pope Innocent II made his call to the Catholic Church to reform itself from wickedness and agreed with the teaching of the Jewish Talmud, the early Church and St. Jerome when about the Tau (Taw) in Yehezqel 9, saying that *"We are called to reform our lives, to stand into the presence of God as righteous people. God will know us by the sign of the tau, T, marked on our foreheads.*" St. Francis of Assisi understood this and with his own call to reform he would outstretch his arms and would tell the Franciscans that their religious habit was in the same shape as the Tau and this meant that they were to be walking crosses. The Eastern Orthodox Christian Community within Israeli Society said, "In the Book of Apocalypsis or Revelation [1:9], the Lord says: "I am the Alpha and Omega, the beginning and the ending"… Jesus Christ did not speak the words of the Gospel Greek. …He certainly had said the Alef and the Tav. The sign of the Tav became the TAU which Saint Francis of Assisi used when blessing Brothers, using the Priestly Blessing [Numbers 22:6]. TAV is a crook and in ancient Hebrew script it had the shape of a cross." The Orthodox Church within Israel recognized the importance of the Taw cross and its historic importance in the ancient Hebrew language. The Greek Tau comes from the Hebrew Taw in shape and name.

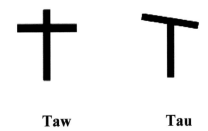

Taw   **Tau**

Chapter 5

Jewish and Christian

Scholars and Resources

As we talk about the cross we must understand that there is a

Hebrew word for cross that is used today in Modern Hebrew. The

Hebrew word for cross is ts'lav (בלצ) and once you understand that

the Jews believed that the sign of God in Yehezqel 9 was in the form

of the ancient Taw cross then the Hebrew word picture seen in ts'lav

(בלצ) makes sense. The Taw cross was God's sign for the righteous

of heart who did not follow after the wicked rulers of Israel. The first

letter used in ts'lav is the Hebrew Tsadik which means a *righteous*

man. The modern shape of the letter is said to represent a person on

their knees with their hands raised to God. The next two letters spell

the word בל lev, which means *a heart.* We can that the Hebrew word

used to describe the cross, the shape of the ancient Taw, is described

in the Hebrew word picture as *The Righteous Heart.* The above

ts'lav is spelled out here from left to right instead of the Hebrew right to left. So we can see that is the by and through the righteous heart of Yeshua (Jesus) that he confirmed the strong covenant of God by dying on the Taw cross. More on the gospel message of the cross will be discussed in chapter 6.

In the New Dictionary by Avraham Eben-Shoshan, who has written one of the most authoritative resources in Israel, he comments on the ancient Canaanite-Hebrew Alef-Bet usage of the final letter Tav. Below is a picture copy of the comment and translated by Dr. Frank T. Seekins in his booklet, The Ancient Tav.

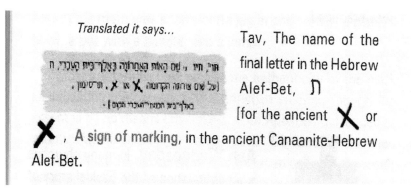

Avraham Rosenstein, later Avraham Eben-Shoshan was born in 1946-1958. Eben-Shoshan compiled *HaMilon HeHadash* (New Dictionary of the Hebrew Language), which became known as the Eben-Shoshan Dictionary. The completed dictionary consisted of 24,698 main entries. He was also the author of the Eben-Shoshan concordance and co-author of the Bialik concordance.

In the Gesenius Hebrew-Chaldee Lexicon to the Old

Testament we have also a reference to the Taw or Tav. Gesenius

explains that in Yehezqel 9:4 (Ezekiel) *a sign*, was in the form of a

cross and the coins of the Maccabees had the form of the cross on

them. Below is a copy of his Lexicon.

תָּו m. (for תָּוֶה), from the root תָּוָה No. 1) –
(1) *a sign*, Eze. 9:4. (Arab. وَسْم . تَوَى a sign in
the form of a cross branded on the thigh or
neck of horses or camels, whence the name
of the letter ת, which in Phoenician, and on
the coins of the Maccabees has the form of
a cross. From the Phoenicians the Greeks
and the Romans took both the name and
form of the letter.)
(2) *sign* (cruciform), *mark* subscribed
instead of a name to a bill of complaint; hence
subscription, Job 31:35. It is state that at
the Synod of Chalcedon and other synods
principally in the East, some even of the
bishops being unable to write, put the sign
of the cross instead of their names, which is
still often done by common people in legal
proceedings; so that in the infancy of the art
of writing this could not fail of being the case,
so as for the expression to be received into
the usage of language.

Heinrich Friedrich Wilhelm Gesenius (3 February 1786 – 23

October 1842) was a German orientalist and Biblical critic. As an exegete he exercised a powerful influence on theological investigation.

Looking also into the different translations of the Bible we can see in their footnotes and commentaries their understanding of the ancient Hebrew letter Taw. Their understanding gives insight into the usage of the ancient letter and how it was know in its original form.

The Douay Rheims version taken from the Vulgate in 1749-1752 shows the same understanding of Taw as Thau or the ancient Hebrew letter shaped like a cross. In Douay Rheims footnote on Yehezqel 9 he states, *"Mark Thau, or Tau, is the last letter in the Hebrew alphabet, and signifies a sign, or a mark; which is the reason why some translators render this place set a mark, or mark a mark, without specifying what this mark was. But St. Jerome, and other interpreters, conclude it was in the form of the letter Thau."* The Douay Rheims footnote concludes the clear understanding and meaning of the ancient Taw cross from the Greek Thau. He references Jerome and other interpreters as having this knowledge as well. The Greek letter Thau was in the shape of a cross like image.

James Martin was a translator for The Commentary of the Old Testament by C.F. Keil and F. Delitzsch. This work is a foundational Protestant commentary. In it we find on Yehezqel 9:4 the following, *"And Jehovah said to him, Go through the midst of the city, through the midst of Jerusalem, and mark a **cross** upon the foreheads of the men who sigh and groan over all the abominations which take place in their midst..."* This foundational commentary clearly uses the cross in its translation of Yehezqel 9:4. The ancient Hebrew letter Taw was still understood to be a cross.

In the New American Bible on this same passage of Yehezqel 9:4 they translate the verse as the following, *"saying to him: Pass through the city (through Jerusalem) and mark an **X** on the foreheads of those who moan and groan over all the abominations that are practiced within it."* The New American Bible then goes on the comment by saying, "An X: literally the Hebrew letter *taw*, which had the form of a cross." To mark an X was to put the letter Taw on the forehead which was the cross. Translation after translation we continue to see the clear understanding of the ancient Hebrew letter Taw. There is no mistaking such a usage of the Taw cross in the Tanakh.

Other Bible translations such as the Darby Bible and the French Jerusalem Bible have the same usage of the Taw cross in Yehezqel 9:4. In the French Jerusalem Bible it says, "a mark of the cross" in French, (et marquee d'une croix). John Darby who was a leader of the Plymouth Brethren and who is considered the father of modern dispensationalism said, "Tau, the name of the last letter of the Hebrew alphabet." Jewish, Catholic and Protestant scholars have taught the ancient Jewish teaching of the Hebrew letter Taw as the shape of the cross and the sign of God on the forehead in Yehezqel 9:4.

This picture of the ancient Taw below was carved in stone about 3800 years ago (300 years before Mosheh aka Moses) at Wadi Al Hol, Egypt.

The cross of our Messiah has been revealed over a thousand years before Yeshua (Jesus). It speaks of God's Word, His love and His protection.

Chapter 6

The Message of the

CROSS

"*For the message of the cross is to them that perish foolishness; but unto us who are saved it is the power of God.*" Sha'ul in Qorintiyim Aleph 1:18 (1 Corinthians 1:18)

In the conclusion of the ancient Hebrew Taw cross we must summarize the message it foretells concerning Yeshua (Jesus) and the redemptive plan of salvation by the fulfillment of the covenant made by God to his people and the world. Let's begin with the Hebrew word "redeem" which in Hebrew is ga'el and looks like this:

The Hebrew letter G (Gamel) means to "lift up" and the next two letters together spell out God (El in singular form). The word picture for "redeem" is "when God is lifted up". This takes us right back to

Yeshua (Jesus) when he said, *"And I, if I am lifted up from the land, will draw all men to Myself...The Son of Man must be lifted up."* These versus spoken by Yeshua (Jesus) in Yohanan 12:32-34 foretell His death in which we are redeemed by His death on the Taw cross. In the language of the Jews, to be lifted up was an expression of being put to death. We see this in verse 34 when the crowd responded to Him. Redemption comes when God is lifted up and since Yeshua is God and came to redeem man by sacrificing Himself for us, we can see how the word picture for "redeem" tells this story. Sha'ul when writing to Titos (Titus) said, *"...who gave himself for us, that he might **redeem** us from all iniquity, and purify unto himself a people for his own possession, zealous of good works."* So we are redeemed because God was lifted up unto death for us, so that we could be saved.

When we consider how God rescued his people out of Egypt we can't forget when got told the Hebrew people to put a sign on the door in blood so death would pass over them. Today this memorial is celebrated by the Jews and it is call The Passover. It is an everlasting Law from generation to generation. Let's take a closer look at the word used for "sign" in ancient Hebrew and see what the word picture tells us. In Shemoth (Exodus) 12:13 we read the following,

*"The blood shall be a **sign** for you on the houses where you live; and when I see the blood I will pass over you, and no plague will befall you to destroy you when I strike the land of Egypt."* The Hebrew word for sign or seal is "oht" אוֹת and begins with aleph then waw and finally the Taw. So what does the sign or seal tell us in the Hebrew word pictures? "The Leader Nailed to the Cross."

Taw   Yod   Aleph

Remember that Aleph means *Leader* and Waw means *Nail* and of course Taw means *Cross*. This is the true word picture meaning of The Passover. As the Hebrews were delivered from death by putting the blood of the lamb over the doorposts, so the blood of Yeshua (Jesus) the true Lamb of God delivers and redeems us from eternal death by His death on the cross. The blood was a sign or a seal for the Hebrews and it is our sign and seal for us today.

We now need to look at the Hebrew words for "Son" and "Covenant". The word *son* in Hebrew is *Bar* in Hebrew and if you add the Hebrew letter Yod to the end it will now become the Hebrew

word for "My Son" or "The Son of." See below for the word picture.

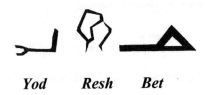

Yod   Resh   Bet

With that in mind we can now add the next Hebrew letter *Taw* to end

next to *Yod* and we will make the Hebrew word Covenant (Breet).

See below for the complete ancient word picture script.

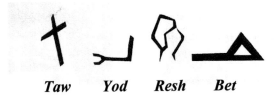

Taw   Yod   Resh   Bet

So what does the word picture for *Covenant* tell us? It says, *"The*

Cross of My Son" or "The Son of the Cross." This ancient Hebrew

word picture for *Covenant* reveals God's son on the cross as the true

and final covenant to man which Yeshua (Jesus) had to fulfill. These

ancient Hebrew word pictures don't contradict what has already

taken place, but only strengthens the message of Yeshua and the

redemptive work on the cross.

God sent the eternal Word and second personage of the

Godhead to become a perfect man in the body of Yeshua (Jesus) to fulfill what the Torah and the prophets had written concerning him,

"They pierced my hands and my feet...and they shall look upon me

(YHWH Yeshua) *whom they have pierce."* Tehillim 22:16 (Psalms)

and Zekaryah 12:10 (Zechariah) Yeshua himself in Luqas (Luke)

24:25-27 said, *"And He said to them, O foolish ones, and slow of*

heart to believe on all things which the prophets spoke! Was it not

necessary for the Christ to suffer these things, and to enter into His

glory? And beginning from Mosheh, and from all the prophets, He

explained to them the things about Himself in all the Scriptures."

The final ancient Hebrew word picture that I would like to

look at is the very covenant name of God. The very name revealed to

Mosheh and the Hebrew people that would be for eternity. The name

Yahweh or YHWH, without the vowels, is the most sacred name in

all of scripture. Modern Jews will not even attempt to pronounce the

name in fear of blasphemy. In some of the earliest writings found in

the Dead Sea scrolls we find written in them the very name of God.

In this passage in Psalms 119:56-64 we see the name below.

When we go back further to the ancient word picture of the name of God we see this: *Hey   Waw   Hey   Yod*

What does this ancient word picture of the name of God tell us? The first Hebrew letter is the *Yod* and means "hand or hands" while the second and last Hebrew letter is the *Hey* and is a picture of a man with his hands upward. This has the meaning also of "lo behold or look" The *Waw* in the middle is of course the "nail" There are several possibilities for a word picture. One could be, "Behold and look at the Nails in my Hands", or "Look at the nails and Behold my Hands" or again, "Behold the Nails in my Hands" No matter how you connect the word picture, one thing is clear, the message is there. Not everyone will agree with the things written in this book but we cannot just dismiss them without examining them. Even if you refuse to accept anything I have written, that will not change the fact that there lived a man name Yeshua (Jesus) who claimed to be the Jewish Messiah and God and who sacrificed himself on the *cross* for what the scriptures call the sins of the world. Confess, Believe and Live.

Resources

Ancient Hebrew Lexicon of the Bible

By Jeff A. Benner

The Ancient Hebrew Language and Alphabet

By Jeff A. Benner

The Ancient Tav

By Dr. Frank T. Seekins

Hebrew Pocket Dictionary

By Ben Yehuda

Hebrew and Chaldee Lexicon

By Friedrich Wilhelm Gesenius (1846)

Hebrew Word Pictures

By Dr. Frank T. Seekins

The New Dictionary

By Avraham Eben-Shoshan

CPSIA information can be obtained
at www.ICGtesting.com
Printed in the USA
LVIC07n2353090913
351731LV00005BB

9 7 8 1 4 6 1 1 3 3 8 9 6